Nine Doors

Vicki Grant

orca currents

ORCA BOOK PUBLISHERS

JAN 15

Library and Archives Canada Cataloguing in Publication

Grant, Vicki
Nine doors / written by Vicki Grant.
(Orca currents)

ISBN 978-1-55469-073-2(pbk.).--ISBN 978-1-55469-074-9 (bound)

I. Title. II. Series: Orca currents
PS8613.R36N55 2009   jC813'.6   C2009-900017-2

First published in the United States, 2009
Library of Congress Control Number: 2008943721

Summary: The game of Nicky Nicky Nine Doors seemed harmless enough when
they started, but Emery and Richard discover there are serious consequences to
scaring your neighbors.

MIX
Paper from
responsible sources
FSC® C004071

ANCIENT FOREST ™
FRIENDLY

*Orca Book Publishers is dedicated to preserving the environment and has
printed this book on Forest Stewardship Council® certified paper.*

Orca Book Publishers gratefully acknowledges the support for its publishing
programs provided by the following agencies: the Government of Canada through
the Canada Book Fund and the Canada Council for the Arts, and the Province of
British Columbia through the BC Arts Council and
the Book Publishing Tax Credit.

Cover image by Firstlight
Author photo by Gus Richardson

ORCA BOOK PUBLISHERS
PO Box 5626, Stn. B
Victoria, BC Canada
V8R 6S4

ORCA BOOK PUBLISHERS
PO Box 468
Custer, WA USA
98240-0468

www.orcabook.com
Printed and bound in Canada.

16 15 14 13 • 6 5 4 3

This book is dedicated to my much older brother, Robert G. Grant, QC, in belated thanks for—among many, many other things—making sure I never lost my retainer.

Prologue

Despite what my math teacher might think, I'm not stupid.

I'm not mean either. At least I try not to be.

So that's not how I got into this mess.

I got into it because I was bored.

I know that's a dumb excuse, but I bet I'm not the first person to use it. My guess is boredom's the reason lots of people get into trouble. It can drive you nuts. It can make you do stuff you'd never do in a million years.

For me, that meant hanging out with Richard.

That sounds cruel, but what can I say? If you knew the guy, you'd probably feel the same way.

There's nothing wrong with him—at least, not really. In fact, it's almost the opposite. Spend more than a couple of minutes with Richard and you end up feeling like there's something wrong with *you*.

I don't know how he does it. He just stands there all innocent and smiling, but somehow he makes you feel like garbage. It's as if the guy's a pickpocket, only he doesn't take your wallet or your cell phone or anything easy like that. He takes your brain. When he's done messing with you, you can't even think straight anymore.

That probably doesn't make any sense. It's kind of hard to explain, but here's an example. Maybe that will help.

My name's Emery. I can't say I love it, but that's my name. Usually, I don't think too much about it one way or the other. It just is.

So one day I ran into Richard down by the Snack 'n Go, and we were having an okay time just talking about music and movies and whatever. I was thinking he's not such a bad guy. He's actually pretty funny. It was the middle of August. Everyone else was away. I figured, why not spend some time with him?

Then, out of the blue, he started calling me Emily. As in, "So, Emily, seen *Scream 12* yet?" Or, "Whoa, nice sneakers, Emily." Just kind of dropping it into conversation like that.

It's not as if Richard's the only person who's ever called me Emily. I got it all the time in elementary school. It used to drive me crazy, but I was just a kid then. Calling me Emily now wasn't going to make me cry or anything. It just bugged me. I let it go a few times, but then I said, "Would you quit it with the Emily stuff?"

He got all serious and said, "Oh. Sorry. I didn't mean to upset you."

I said, "You didn't upset me. I'm just saying don't call me Emily." I said it in my normal voice. I didn't scream or anything. I just kind of "stated" it, if you know what I mean.

He raised his eyebrows way up. He took a step back and said, "Okay, okay," as if I was making a big deal about it.

Where did that come from? I looked at him for a second. I wasn't sure how to react. If I said anything more, I figured it really *would* look like I was turning it into a big deal.

He bit the side of his lip and turned away as if he suddenly just had to read the Ice Blaster poster in the store window. I couldn't tell if he was laughing at me or not, but I wouldn't have been surprised. I got the distinct feeling he was *trying* to bug me—which, of course, just bugged me more.

I took a big breath. I could feel my whole face twisting up into a knot. I felt like calling him Ricky or Rachel or Jerk and seeing how much he liked that.

A couple of seconds later, he turned around as if nothing had happened. I was all ready to let it go. I mean, I'm a reasonable guy. I'm not looking for trouble.

Then he started calling me Emery.

Emery, this. Emery, that. Over and over again. He made a point of really laying into that middle syllable every time he said it too. It was my own name, but somehow Richard managed to make it sound even more irritating than when he was calling me Emily.

If the owner of the Snack 'n Go hadn't come out right then and told us to move along, I seriously think I would have hauled off and punched Richard.

I've never punched anyone before in my life!

See what I mean about the guy?

Richard makes you think things you don't want to think, do things you don't want to do. He's always twisting stuff around in your head. It's like he Photoshops reality right in front of you, and you still get tricked into believing his version's the real thing.

Sure I was bored, but I knew Richard was like that right from the start. I knew I should have kept my distance. I knew I shouldn't have let him weasel his way into my brain.

I guess that makes me as much to blame as he is for what happened next.

Door Number One

It all started out innocently enough.

A few days later, I was riding my bike around the neighborhood just for something to do. I saw Richard come out of his house. I was only going to say hi and keep moving, but somehow we started talking about school and the closing ceremonies. Richard did this hilarious impression of Mr. Moffatt tripping over the microphone cord and practically flattening Kalli Harvey. (He did a pretty good impression of Kalli too. She's usually so perfect that we were all shocked to hear her swear like that.)

Next thing I knew we were hanging out for the day.

We rode our bikes for a while. Then we went to the Snack 'n Go for a slushie. The owner doesn't like you "loitering" after you've finished your food, so we went to the playground. Where else was there to go?

What a barrel of fun that was. The monkey bars were gone because a couple of parents had complained that they weren't safe anymore. Most of the other equipment was busted or boring. A bunch of old people doing tai chi had taken over the field. That didn't leave much for us to do. We found a tree behind the school and chilled in the shade.

It was hot and sticky. The whole subdivision smelled like a bus terminal or a parking lot or something. I just wanted to go to sleep and wake up when things got fun again.

"Hey, I got an idea," Richard said. He pitched a couple of pebbles at my face. "Let's play Nicky Nicky Nine Doors!"

I was lying on the dry crunchy grass, trying to remember what cool felt like. I didn't even bother to open my eyes.

I blew the pebbles off my face and said, "Nicky Nicky what?" I made sure my voice sounded bored. If the game was even half as stupid as the name, I wasn't interested.

"Nicky Nicky Nine Doors," he said. "You know, when you ring someone's doorbell and then run off before they answer it."

I rolled over on my stomach and bugged my eyes out at him.

"You mean Ding Dong Ditch? Ring and Run? That thing?"

He nodded at me like "Won't that be great?"

What was he, six years old or something? That game was so pathetic.

"Why would you want to do that?" I said.

He flicked a pebble off his knee and nailed me right in the forehead. It was little, but it hurt. "Got anything better to do?" he said.

He had a point. I was sick of riding my bike. The public pool would be crawling with toddlers, no doubt all peeing their little hearts out. My mother barred me from the house on sunny days because I was playing too many video games. I couldn't even go to a movie because I'd blown all my money on slushies.

"Well...?" Richard said. "Any other brilliant ideas?"

I got up before he had a chance to ding me with another pebble.

"No," I said.

"So you're in?" he said.

What could it hurt? If nothing else, I figured, it would kill some time.

Kill is right. Nicky Nicky Nine Doors was even more boring than lying in the shade watching old people pretend they're Jackie Chan. I hid behind a parked car and waited while Richard rang a bunch of doorbells.

Nobody answered.

Big surprise. Who was going to answer? The subdivision was practically empty these days. The kids were all away at camp or on vacation or visiting their "noncustodial" parent. Most of the grown-ups worked in the city. They were never around anyway.

After the third or fourth doorbell, I was pretty sure Richard would be ready to give up. That just goes to show how little I knew him.

He ran back from the last house and slid down behind the car with me. "Okay," he said. "Who else can we try?"

I shrugged.

He went, "Oh, come on. You live on this street. You must know who's home during the day."

I shook my head.

"You do so," he said.

"No, I don't," I said. "I don't know anybody on the street." It was just that kind of place. Most people kept to themselves.

Richard squeezed his lips together and looked at me over the top of his glasses. It was like he was a teacher and I'd just given him some bogus excuse for not getting my homework done. "You've been living here a couple of years and you don't know *anybody*? On the *entire* street? Hmmm," he said. "That's funny."

He made me feel like I was lying.

I sighed. "Okay. Well, yeah. I guess I know a couple of people."

"There. That's better. Thank you, Emery. Now, who might those people be?"

I wasn't going to let him see how much he was irritating me. I ran my tongue over my teeth. I looked up and down the street in the laziest way I could.

I jerked my head toward a house that was exactly like ours except for the red door. "Mr. Henkel or Hinkel or something lives there, but he's away until August twenty-fifth. I only know that because I'm looking after his cat."

"Excellent, Emery! You're doing very well. And who else?" Richard smiled at me. It was one of those insulting smiles, the kind you'd give someone who has trouble tying his own shoelaces or saying the alphabet in order. I rubbed my nose with the back of my hand and tried not to let it get to me.

I pointed at the house attached to ours. "There's an old lady living there, but I don't know her. I've never even met her. I think her name's Marjorie or something." Just as I said it, we saw someone move behind the lacy curtain in the living-room window.

Richard's eyes perked up.

"Perfect. Our first victim. Nyah-ha-ha." He laughed like the evil genius he was.

"No," I said. "No way. She's sick. There's something the matter with her. She never comes out of the house. Mom would kill me if we did anything to her."

I could see Richard searching his brain for some excuse that would make it okay to pick on a sick old lady, but he didn't come up with anything.

"Fine," he said, making it very clear that he didn't think it was fine at all. "Who else is there then?"

"That's it," I said. "The only other person I know is my mother—but don't even think about it. You aren't ringing our doorbell. She's trying to get this big article finished for some magazine and, trust me, she would not find the interruption funny."

Richard leaned his head to one side. "Oh yeah? She might…Never know until you try!"

Was he joking, or was he really going to do it? You never could tell with Richard. He has one of those baby faces that adults think are so adorable. They see the big blue eyes, the curly blond hair, the smart-kid glasses, and they just can't imagine him doing anything wrong. I wasn't that easily fooled.

It crossed my mind that I should let him go ahead and ring our doorbell after all. Sicking my mother on him would sure pay him back for all the times he'd bugged me. (The guy would be having nightmares about it for years.)

No. I couldn't be that cruel.

I was just going to say, "Let's forget about the stupid game," when a door down the street opened. This chunky guy came out and shook a blanket over the railing. He was wearing a pink flowered apron with a bow in the back. It even had those frilly things on the shoulders.

Richard's face scrunched up into this big grin. I swear he looked exactly like the Grinch. He rubbed his hands together. "Well, well, well," he said. "Looky here…I think it's time we paid Mr. Mom a little visit, don't you?"

I have to admit I laughed. I mean, if you're going to ring somebody's doorbell, you want to ring the doorbell of a big beefy guy in a pink flowered apron.

Seriously.

His outfit would have made a great Halloween costume, but it was a little bizarre for a Tuesday afternoon in

August. He was right out of some bad sitcom. All he needed was a blond wig and a pair of high-heeled shoes with pompoms on the toes.

We waited until the guy went back inside, and then we snuck closer to his house. It's weird. I'd have been really embarrassed if any of my friends caught me playing something called Nicky Nicky Nine Doors, but right then, it didn't matter. I was actually starting to feel kind of excited. I had to bite my lip to stop from laughing.

I crouched down behind another car. I felt like a cop staking out a suspect in some action movie. Richard checked to make sure the coast was clear, then "casually" strolled across the street and up the guy's front stairs. He did another quick look around, then rang the doorbell. He must have held it down for five or six seconds before he booted it back to our hiding place.

We peeked up through the car window and held our breath. You'd think Richard had just planted a bomb or something—that's how wound up we were.

We waited and waited. Nothing happened.

All of a sudden, Richard banged his hand against the car window. "What's the matter with the guy? Is he deaf or something? We know he's in there! He can't hide."

I was sort of startled. I don't think I'd ever seen Richard mad before. He always acted like nothing bothered him.

He slumped back down against the side of the car, all dejected.

"So try again, why don't you?" I said. I knew he really wanted to get the guy, but that wasn't the only reason I encouraged him. Somehow I wasn't just killing time anymore. It was my game now too. I wanted to see what happened as much as he did.

I elbowed Richard in the ribs. "Come on!" I said. "Try again. He was probably just touching up his mascara or couldn't hear you over the hair dryer or something."

Richard liked that. He sort of chuckled. "Right. That was probably it."

He pointed at me and winked. "This time, he'll hear me for sure." He did a quick scan of the area. He dropped his voice way down low. "Cover me. I'm going in!"

He darted across the street, all hunched over like a commando under heavy fire. He slid up the stairs with his back against the wall, then rang the bell. He pressed his ear to the door and listened. After a while, he turned toward me and lifted his hands up in a shrug. No one was coming. I motioned at him to ring the bell again.

This time he pushed it for a really long time. He waited. When there was no answer, he pushed it again.

And again.

And again.

He dropped the whole commando thing and started doing this little dance. My guess is he was tapping out some song on the doorbell. His moves were unbelievably lame. It was like something my dad would do in one of his many embarrassing attempts to look cool. It totally cracked me up. That's one thing you've got to like about Richard. He'll do anything for a laugh.

All of a sudden, his eyes flew open. He jumped down the stairs and booted it across the street, flapping his hands in front of him like a little kid who'd just seen a monster. I couldn't tell if he was trying to be funny or if he really was scared. Either way, it was hilarious. He dove down behind the car just as the door opened.

The guy said, "Hello? Hello…?" He stepped out of the house and looked around. He was way older than I'd thought he was. I got the impression he used to be a cop once upon a time. He had the look down pat—the slicked-back hair, the bulging arms, the gray pants with the crease down the middle. (The apron, of course, watered down the whole macho thing he had going on.)

It only took the guy a couple of seconds to realize someone was playing a prank on him. Even through the car windows, we could see how mad he was. His face had gone pinker than his apron. He did this angry Ninja thing with his mouth. I was working so hard not to laugh I was afraid my brain was going to start spurting out my ears.

The guy called out, "Just wait until I get my hands on you kids! So help me, I'm going to…I'm going to…" Either he couldn't find the words or he figured they were too rude to scream out in the middle of the day. He tore his apron off and threw it on the porch. It would have looked like a real tough-guy thing to do if had been a bulletproof vest or a flack jacket, but frankly, under the circumstances, it was just funny.

He must have seen us move or heard us snort or something, because suddenly he looked up. He started coming down the stairs straight for us. I have to admit it made me nervous. He was a lot scarier without the apron on.

I was sure we were toast.

But then the guy suddenly turned around and went, "No, no. It's all right, Norma. It's nothing. I'm coming." He sounded all sweet as pie again.

He snatched the apron up off the porch. He went back into the house. Just before he closed the door, he leaned out and shook his fist in our general direction.

We thought it was the most comical thing we'd ever seen.

At least we did at the time.

Later, of course, it wasn't so funny.

Door Number Two

I was only joking when I said, "Too bad we didn't get that on videotape."

Lesson Number One: Never joke with Richard.

The next thing I knew we weren't playing Nicky Nicky Nine Doors anymore. We were making *Nicky Nicky Nine Doors: The Movie*.

"Seriously," Richard said. "This could be our big break! Critics love this sort of thing. You know: 'Fourteen-year-old boys make ground-breaking documentary.' I'm not kidding. We could go to all the film festivals. Meet all the big stars. Make a ton of money…"

I was rolling my eyes, but I was sort of going for it too. I mean, how cool would that be? Making our own movie. Getting famous. Getting rich. I acted reluctant, but I was totally up for it.

I had to do an errand for my mother. By the time I got back an hour later, Richard had scrounged a video camera and had practically written the script too.

"Okay, this is what we should do," he said. "We'll stick to this street. We'll ring nine doors and videotape what happens. Then afterwards, we'll go back and explain that we're making a movie. We'll interview the people. You know, ask them how they felt when nobody was there. Ask them if they played the same game when they were kids. Whatever…"

Hearing him describe our so-called "blockbuster" kind of killed my enthusiasm. "I don't know," I said. "It sounds a little boring. *We* might find it funny, but I'm not sure anybody else would."

I tried to be as gentle as I could—I didn't want to hurt his feelings—but I mean, come on. Interviewing people? It sounded like one of those educational films you watch in social studies class.

Richard was already rooting around in his backpack for the video camera, so I wasn't expecting him to take my comments very well—but he surprised me. He tapped his finger on his front tooth and nodded. "You're right," he said. "It is kind of lame. We need to add something else…get a little excitement in there…"

He paced back and forth for a while and then sat down on the lawn to think.

"Whoa! Watch it!" I said. I pointed to a crusty brown mound on the grass right next to where he was sitting.

He put on this appalled-old-lady voice and went, "Ewww! Doggie droppings! How positively vile!"

The natural thing to do was to move away. It was a hot day. Believe me, you don't want to be around a pile of "droppings" on a hot day. I took a few steps back—but not Richard. He was down on his knees, staring at the stuff as if he'd just discovered a new life-form or something.

"I got to get this on film!" he said.

I managed to cough out, "*Why*?"

Although, frankly, I really didn't want to know the answer.

Richard rubbed his chin and smiled. "What can I say? Different things inspire different people. Isaac Newton had the apple. I've got...this!" He waved his hand at the pile as if he was introducing the lead singer in his band.

He turned on the camera and leaned in for the close-up.

I practically gagged.

"What are you *doing*?" I said.

"Just documenting the process, my friend," he said. "This humble pile of bio-waste has inspired me to undertake... the Flaming Feces project!"

I went, "I have no idea what you're talking about."

"Bio-waste? You know—doggy-doo, canine ca-ca..."

"I know what it is! I just don't understand how it could have inspired you—or anybody else, for that matter."

He took the camera away from his face and sighed. I guess I was being dense.

"Please. It's the oldest trick in the book! You put the fecal matter in a brown paper bag. You place the brown paper bag on the porch. You light the bag on fire. You ring the doorbell. You run. When the homeowner opens the door, they see the fire. They put it out with the first thing they can find—which, generally speaking, is their foot." He let this sink in for a second.

I got it. I laughed. He was right. It was a funny idea.

This wicked smile spread over that angelic face of his.

"If we're *really* lucky," he said, "they'll remember the immortal words of the fire safety pledge…"

I knew exactly where he was going with this. We both said it together.

"Stop, drop and roll!"

We cracked up. The image of that guy in his apron rolling over a flaming doggie bag was just too much for me.

I was laughing so hard I didn't even notice Richard had moved on to other things. He'd pulled a paper bag out of his knapsack. He dumped the Choco-Nutz bar inside it onto the ground.

"You just *happen* to have a paper bag with you?" I said, wiping the tears from my eyes.

"Yeah. So?" He made it sound like the most natural thing in the world. "I'm a good Boy Scout—always prepared."

He picked up a couple of twigs as if they were chopsticks and started trying to drop the poop into the bag. (It was harder than it sounds.) "Shall we give it a go?" he said.

"What? No!" I said. "You're not actually serious!"

He stuck his neck out at me. "Why not? You seemed to think it was funny."

"Yeah, but…" I just looked at him with my mouth hanging open. I didn't know where to start. Setting fire to a bag of doggie droppings was just so wrong on so many levels.

"Ye-es?" He said it like a challenge, as if only an idiot would disagree with him.

"Okay, for starters…," I said but then had to stop. "Would you quit playing with it for a second so I can think straight?" Seriously. What was wrong with the guy? He was like a kid with a new tub of play dough.

He said, "Oooh, sorry," under his breath and then stuck the twigs into the mound like two little antlers. "I didn't realize you were so sensitive."

I let that go. I tried again. "Okay. For starters, it's full of germs. It's gross!"

"That's the whole point!" he went. "All the popular movies are gross. That's what makes them funny!"

He snorted at my stupidity. I snorted right back.

"Movies aren't gross. They just *look* gross. Newsflash, Richard: It's make-believe. They use props. You think Adam

Sandler or Will Ferrell would actually roll around in…in…that?" I pointed.

Richard looked down and smiled at the pile as if it was too cute to actually do any harm. After a while he shrugged and went, "Okay, fine. No biggie. So we won't use it."

He smiled.

"We'll use stunt poo instead."

I laughed—but Richard was apparently serious. He picked the chocolate bar off the grass and unwrapped it. It was starting to melt. He squished it with his hands and kind of bent it so it wasn't perfect. He put it on the grass beside the real thing. If you knew what it was, it still looked like a chocolate bar, but if you didn't…

Now I really laughed.

"So," he said, licking the chocolate off his hands. "Problem solved?"

"No," I said. "You're still lighting it on fire. That's dangerous."

Richard threw back his head and groaned. "Look. Do you want to make a movie or don't you?"

"Yeah, I do. I just don't want to—"

He cut me off. "Well, then get used to it. Nobody pays to go to a *Batman* movie to watch the Joker double-park. People want danger! They want excitement!"

I didn't say anything. Who did he think he was kidding? Burning bio-waste was gross, but frankly, it wasn't that exciting. I'd rather watch a car chase any day.

He waved his hand at me. "Oh, come on," he went. "These are brick houses, cement steps, asphalt driveways. What could possibly catch on fire?"

"I don't know. Lots," I said. "Frankly, I don't want to go to jail because I burnt down somebody's house playing"—I paused so he could hear how dumb it sounded—"Nicky Nicky Nine Doors."

I turned to go.

Richard went, "All right. All right. You win." He picked up the bag and tore the top half off.

"Okay," he said. "How about this? Stunt poo, itty-bitty bag and a bucket of water to put out the flames. Does that meet your safety requirements, Fire Chief Murray?"

I looked at the bag. It was half the size of my shoe. I felt ridiculous. How much harm could a little thing like that do?

I hesitated. I didn't want to look like a wuss.

"Okay, okay!" he said. "I'll also throw in a fire truck and—for a limited time only—a Dalmatian dog wearing a little red helmet too!"

I laughed. What could I do?

"Fine," I said. "Whatever."

"Excellent!" Richard plopped the chocolate bar into the paper bag and dug around in his backpack for matches. That's when I knew I'd been tricked.

The doggie-doo.

The bag.

The chocolate bar.

The matches.

Some inspiration. My guess is Richard had this planned right from the start. I could just see him planting the dog poop there himself. The weird thing is, I almost admired him for it. The guy sure knew how to get what he wanted.

"Now," he said, "we just have to find a victim…"

He turned on the camera and started playing with the controls. "Nice," he said. "You can zoom right into people's windows. Take a look."

I peered at our house through the camera. I could see my mother pounding away on her computer. I scanned past Marjorie's place. I saw something move inside, but the curtains were closed so I couldn't tell if it was her or a cat or just the wind. The next few houses seemed empty—but the one at the end was better than we could have hoped for.

I passed the camera back to Richard. "See the house on the corner?" I said. "There's someone on the second floor… left-hand side."

I waited while he zeroed in on them.

"If the house is laid out like ours," I said, "the person's in the bathroom."

I didn't need to explain. Richard understood immediately.

He put on that old-lady voice again. "Oh dear, oh dear. I do hope we shan't be catching them at an inconvenient time…" He did this ha-ha chuckle thing.

"Oh and look, Nervous Nelly," he said. "You're in luck. There's a hose at the side of the house. That's even better than a bucket."

We crept down behind a car. He handed me the camera and looked right into the lens. He spoke in the whispery way reporters do when they're trying to sound important.

"Door number two. The prey has been spotted. All systems are go. Now it's up to yours truly—the fearless Richard B. Inkpen—to deliver the blow."

He poked his face up like a periscope, did a quick check for witnesses and then booked it across the street.

He ran to the side of the house and pulled the hose over to the steps. He made this big deal of turning on the tap and demonstrating how the water spurted out. He gave me a cheesy thumbs-up, then tiptoed up the stairs.

This time he didn't take any chances. He rang the bell a bunch of times and waited until he heard someone coming. He leaned down, lit the bag on fire and disappeared around beside the steps.

The door opened, and the all-time hairiest guy I've ever seen stepped out, wearing nothing but a white towel. He looked around for a second before he noticed the fire. He followed the script exactly.

He stomped on it with his bare foot.

He screamed.

His towel fell off and landed on the fire.

He stood there buck naked for a second—just long enough for me to get a clear shot. Then he picked up the flaming towel and ran back into the house.

We just lost our PG-13 rating, but that didn't matter.

It made amazing footage.

Door Number Three

Watching Naked Guy try to put out the fire was what did it for me. Suddenly, I was convinced our movie was going to win an Oscar. I didn't want to miss my chance at stardom. It was my turn to ring the doorbell.

We scoped the neighborhood for another target. I noticed signs of life in a house at the far end of the dead-end street. Richard got the bag ready, then ran me through the procedure.

My heart was pounding as if I was about to jump off the high diving board, but Richard didn't need to know that.

"Yeah, yeah," I said. "I got it. It's not that hard."

I grabbed the bag and the matches from him. I said, "You ready?"

He nodded, held the camera up to his eye and then went, "Aaand…Action!"

I took off across the street. I almost tripped on my shoelace, but there was no way I was stopping to tie it. I stumbled up the steps. I put the bag on the welcome mat and lit a match.

A breeze blew it out.

I tried again—but this time I put the match out myself. What was I thinking? The mat was made of straw or something. If a spark landed on it, it would go up in flames for sure. That's all I needed.

I pushed the mat out of the way. The people who lived there had obviously been using it to cover a big crack in the concrete. I put the bag back down on the porch. My hands were shaking so hard by now I had to light four matches before one worked.

The bag whooshed up into flames. I didn't expect such a big fire. It made me jump. I knew Richard must have been laughing his face off at that, but I couldn't let it bother me. I pulled myself together and rang the doorbell.

I wanted to take off right then, but I didn't. No way was I going to run if Richard hadn't run. I didn't want to look like a chicken. I put my ear up to the door and listened.

A couple of seconds passed. No sound. I rang again.

Bingo.

Almost right away, I heard footsteps bouncing down the stairs.

I turned to run—and almost fell flat on my face. I jerked my leg forward but couldn't move my right foot. I looked down. My shoelace was stuck in the crack in the concrete. I tried to pull it free, but the knot at the end was rammed in there good.

Someone inside said, "Coming! Coming!" Even if I'd taken my shoe off right away, I'd still have been nailed. I had no time to run.

That stupid bag was still burning. I suddenly remembered I didn't get the hose ready. Lot of good it would do me now.

I had to put the fire out before I got caught.

I blew on the bag. That just fed the flame.

I thought about throwing the whole thing into the bushes, but I canned that idea pretty quick. The weather had been so dry lately that the place would burn down for sure.

The lock on the door clicked open.

Why was the bag taking so long to go out? You'd swear it was the Olympic flame or something. A thought flashed through my mind. Richard probably stuffed the bag full of extra paper when I wasn't looking. He might have even soaked it in lighter fluid for all I knew. I wouldn't have put it past him.

I tried to spit on it, but my mouth had gone completely dry. That always happens when I'm in trouble.

The hinges squeaked. The door was opening.

The fire was still burning. I did the only thing I could think of doing. Not quite "stop, drop and roll" but close enough.

I sat on it. The fire went out with a little puff and a whistling sound.

Someone said, "Hello?"

I looked up. This girl with long black hair was standing there looking down at me.

She had the brownest eyes I'd ever seen. She scrunched them up as if to say, "What are you doing?" (Or maybe she was asking, "Why is there smoke coming out your pants?") I put my hands up like "I don't know." I must have looked ridiculous. She shook her head. Then she kind of smiled.

I tried to smile back, but you wouldn't believe how hot that chewy caramel filling suddenly was. I started to worry I was doing serious damage to myself. Some day I wanted to have children.

"Is something the matter?" she said.

"No. Um…It's just…," I said.

This loud voice from inside the house went, "What's burning? Is something burning, Bebi?" The guy had a really thick accent.

I looked at her, all panicky, and shook my head. I whispered, "No! No!"

I could see the girl wasn't sure if she should help me or not, but I mouthed the word *Pleeeease* in the most pathetic way I could. She pretended to look mad at me for a second, but then she said, "No, Dad, it's nothing."

That didn't stop him from coming to take a look for himself. He obviously wasn't too impressed to find me sitting on the porch like that. I would have stood up, but I didn't know what kind of mess I'd leave behind.

"I smell something," her father said.

The girl shrugged and shook her head like she had no idea what he was talking about.

"I don't," she said. Then she looked at me. "Do you?"

I shook my head too—but just gently. I was trying to keep myself out of the boiling caramel as best I could. Any movement at all was proving painful.

Her dad looked back and forth between the two of us. He clearly thought we were up to something. He started talking to her in a language I didn't recognize.

"Dad!" she said. "You're wrong. He's in science camp with me! He's one of the kids on the team."

Her father said something else. She sighed and went, "Because he came a long way, that's why! He's tired. Right... um, Donald?"

I figured that was me. I nodded.

"Yeah," I said, "it's been a long day." That much was true.

Her father tilted his head and looked at her with one eye. She didn't even blink. He shook his finger at her and then said something. She went, "Da-ad! You're so suspicious. Like it's a crime to sit on someone's porch!"

He went into the house. She got this embarrassed look on her face and said, "Sorry about that."

I couldn't believe it. She was apologizing to *me*? It was almost funny.

I said, "No. No. I'm the one who should be sorry."

She was already closing the door. She said, "I better go," and then in a louder voice so her father could hear, "I'll find that book and bring it for you tomorrow, Donald."

I hoped she meant it. For a second, I almost forgot I wasn't in science camp with her. I really wanted to see her again.

The door clicked shut. She peeked out the window and gave one of those little twiddly waves with her fingers.

I stood up. The chocolate bar—or at least what was left of it—had started to harden. These gross gooey strings of dirty brown caramel went from the porch to the back of my pants. I could just imagine what it looked like. (Bebi probably had never heard of stunt poo.) I backed down the stairs—and all the way across the street.

Richard was laughing so hard it sounded like he was having an asthma attack.

I didn't care. Let him laugh. I didn't even mind the pain anymore.

I was thinking about Bebi.

Door Number Four

I've never seen Richard happier. He had this big grin on his face, and his eyes were bouncing around like bugs in a jar. He looked as if he'd thrown back a few too many energy drinks.

He went, "This is SO great! Like, I mean, seriously. So great. We've got violence…We've got nudity…We've even got a hot girl. All we need now is a big musical number, and it's a wrap, folks!" He slapped his cheek in utter amazement at our brilliant creation.

Me? I didn't really care about the movie anymore. The only doorbell I wanted to ring now was Bebi's.

I think Richard guessed what was up. He snapped his fingers in front of my face and went, "Hey, yo! Earth to Loverboy. Let's get moving! We've got lots more doors to do. And since you just proved yourself to be a master of slapstick humor, I think you should do the honors again."

My heart wasn't really in it, but I said, "Yeah, okay." I figured the sooner we got this done, the sooner I could see Bebi again. Maybe I could find out what camp she was going to and sign myself up. My mother would be thrilled if I suddenly decided I wanted to study science for a week. She didn't like me "hanging around doing nothing all summer." Little did she know.

Richard was looking through the camera. "I've scanned the whole neighborhood. As far as I can tell, there's only one possibility at the moment."

"Yeah?" I said. "What's that?"

"Your place," he said.

That woke me up. "No!" I said. "No way. I told you we aren't hitting my house!" He started doing that ha-ha chuckle thing again. He loved getting a reaction out of me.

Mom was standing at the window with a coffee in her hand. She saw us looking and waved. She'd kill me if she knew what we were doing. She hates "boneheaded" pranks.

We waved back. "She doesn't seem that scary to me," Richard said. He put on that innocent voice of his. "Seriously. Are you afraid of her? Is that the problem?" He leaned toward me as if this would be our little secret.

I looked at him with my eyes half-open and said, "No," in the flattest voice I could. I stuck my hands in my pockets and acted bored.

Richard had this smirk on his face. He raised his eyebrow as if he didn't believe me. I ignored him. He'd have to find some other way to bug me. He turned away.

"Hey, look!" he said. "I think the old lady's watching us again." He pointed at Marjorie's house and gave this big beauty-queen wave. What a jerk.

I checked to see if Marjorie saw. There was no one in the window. I looked at Richard. He just smiled. It would have seemed innocent enough to anyone else, but he didn't fool me. I got the feeling he was up to something. I was pretty sure I knew what it was.

Talking with Richard was like playing hockey with this kid I know. I can be

one-hundred-percent sure that Tommy
Grant is going to go one way with the
puck—then he'll deke past me the other
way. It works every time. He always
scores on me.

I was willing to bet Richard was
trying to do the same thing. Pretending
to go one way when he was actually
planning to go the other.

He didn't really want to get my
mother. She was just a normal, boring,
middle-aged woman. Who'd want to
watch her in a movie? (No offence,
Mom.)

What Richard wanted was a sick
old lady. It would make much more
interesting footage—especially if she
was creepy or cranky or, even better,
clearly insane.

My guess is Richard figured that if
he bugged me enough about hitting up
our place, I'd break down and agree to
do Marjorie's instead. I can't be sure

that's what he was thinking, but it made sense in a weird sort of way.

I was wondering if I should say anything to him about it when a car pulled into a driveway down the street. Richard forgot about Marjorie. He had a new victim.

A lady got out, carrying a big pile of groceries. She must have gone in and out of the house about four times before she had everything unloaded. She propped the door open with a bag of potatoes and went back to the car. She took out two babies—twins, I guess. She had one in each arm. They weren't very happy. They kicked and screamed and slammed her in the face all the way into the house. (I take back what I said before about wanting to have kids.)

We waited until she was inside for a few minutes before we struck.

I ran up the steps, lit the bag and rang the doorbell. The kids started howling again immediately. I gave the bell another ring, just to make sure, then slipped down beside the stairs where the hose was.

Despite everything I just said about not wanting to do the movie anymore, I was excited again. I was thinking this scene could be pretty funny. I was also thinking how impressed Bebi would be when she found out we were making a film.

The door opened. The sound of the babies' screeching made me want to cover my ears. I wondered if the camera mike would pick up the noise or if we'd have to add sound effects later.

I expected the lady to go into a big panic over the fire but she didn't. She didn't scream or jump around or anything. She didn't even try to put it out.

She just slumped down on the edge of the step, put her face in her hands and started to cry.

Door Number Five

It was the saddest thing I ever saw.

I felt so bad. I felt like I'd pushed that poor lady right over the edge. I mean, what was I thinking? It was pretty obvious she already had enough to handle with four tons of groceries and two maniac babies. Did she really need me ringing her doorbell right then? It wasn't even funny. It was just cruel.

"Oh, lighten up!" Richard said. "It's only a game! Give her a couple of days. By then, she'll be laughing about it."

He could tell by the look on my face that I didn't buy it. He got all serious.

He said, "Or maybe this little incident will actually help her. Who knows? It could turn out to be the thing that finally pushes her to get the mental help she so clearly needs."

He waited a couple of seconds just so he didn't appear totally heartless, and then he shrugged. "Either way, it's going to make an excellent segment. It's a nice change of pace. It adds a little heartache. That's what people want in films: the full range of human experience."

Who did he think he was? Some big-time movie producer? As if he knew everything. As if giving some poor lady a nervous breakdown was okay because it's all part of "the full range of human experience." It was enough to make me barf.

He picked up the camera. "Okay. My turn!" He focused in on a house a few doors down. "Hmmm...I thought this one was empty, but I'm pretty sure I just saw some movement. I'm going to give it a try."

He handed me back the camera. "You ready?" he said.

No, I wasn't. I didn't want to play the stupid game anymore. I felt bad for that lady. And, come to think of it, I was also feeling kind of bad for Naked Guy and the guy in the apron too. I wasn't sure how comical any of them would find our little game.

So why didn't I just tell Richard, "I quit"?

I was all ready to. I opened my mouth. I took a breath. But before I could say anything, he went, "I hope this is as good as the scene you did with that girl. Even half as good! I mean it. That was amazing!"

He was so excited. He was like a little kid about to open a big birthday present or something. It was almost sad. As much as I wanted to, I couldn't snatch it away from him now.

That was the thing about Richard. On one hand, it was like he had some power over me. He could talk me into doing all sorts of things I didn't want to do. On the other hand, I felt kind of sorry for him, like he was my dopey little brother or something. I had to protect him, look after him. I had this feeling I was the only friend he had.

Maybe *that's* the power he had over me. What could I do?

I sighed. "Yeah, okay. I'm ready."

Richard ran across the street and rang the bell. A second later, this big, black pit bull came flying out from the backyard, barking its ugly, beady-eyed face off. If its leash had been even a centimeter longer, Richard would have lost his leg.

The dog was lunging and snapping at him as if it hadn't eaten in a month.

Richard was too scared to even scream. He practically dove across the street. He lay there panting with his back against the car. He was white and sweaty, and shaking as if he was caught in the middle of his own personal little earthquake.

The very first thing he said was, "Did you get it? Did you get that on tape?"

The guy barely escaped with his life, but that's all he could think of. The movie. You've got to laugh.

And we did. For quite a long time—especially after we noticed the big tooth marks in Richard's pant leg.

We stopped dead, though, when we noticed a cop car pull up in front of Naked Guy's house. My first thought was, This is bad.

Richard thought the same thing—but that's the difference between us.

For Richard, bad is good. He grabbed the camera from me and started shooting.

We couldn't hear what the guy was saying to the cops, but I was pretty sure he was talking about us. He pointed to a spot on the porch and then threw his hands up in the air. You could tell he was mad. The female cop rubbed her boot back and forth over the concrete and wrote something in a little notebook. They shook hands with the guy, and then the cops started walking down the steps.

"Let's get out of here!" I said. Richard didn't move. He didn't even stop shooting. I grabbed the camera from him and started walking back toward my house as fast as I could. I would have run, but I figured that would have given me away.

I heard, "Boys! Excuse me! Boys!" It was still really hot out, but suddenly I was cold all over.

We turned around. The male cop was smiling at us. He waved us over.

Those were the longest ten steps of my life.

"Mind if we have a word with you fellas?" he said.

He looked me right in the eye and put his hands on his hips. He had a big black club hanging off his belt. He said, "You wouldn't know anything about some fires being set around here, would you?"

If he'd turned his head even three centimeters to the right, he'd have seen the paper bag and matches that Richard had left behind the car.

"Ah, no, officer," I said. My voice came out higher than it usually did. It didn't even sound like a boy's voice— or a girl's voice, for that matter. It just sounded like a liar's voice.

"Me neither," Richard said. His voice was higher too—but higher the way a little kid's is. An innocent little kid. I got the feeling he made it sound like that on purpose. If I hadn't known any better, I would have thought Richard was about eight years old. The guy had morphed right before my eyes.

I suddenly knew I didn't stand a chance. Who were the cops going to blame? The tall skinny guy with the camera and the big I'm-guilty chocolate stain on his pants? Or the little curly-headed kid who looks like he's just waiting for his babysitter to come get him?

The female cop raised her eyebrows way up and went, "Hmmm…" What did she mean by that?

"You're sure?" the other cop said.

We said, "Yeah."

He pushed back his cap and looked at me for a while. Then he went, "Well, okay." He pulled a card out of his pocket. "This is my number. If you hear of anyone setting fires around here, give me a call. It hasn't rained in weeks. I'd hate a fire to start just because a game got out of hand…"

I nodded and smiled before I realized this might not be the appropriate time to smile, so I just nodded again. I knew the more I fussed, the guiltier I looked, but I couldn't help it. I didn't know what to do with my face.

The cops turned to go. They were already getting in the cruiser when the female cop said, "And one more thing you should know, guys—arson is a very serious charge."

We kind of stood at attention on the side of the road until their car disappeared. Then Richard cracked up. I glared at him. I didn't find this funny at all. I started walking home.

"What? What's your problem?" he said. "That was hysterical! That was great!"

"No, it wasn't," I said. "That was the end. I'm finished. I'm not doing this anymore."

"Oh, come on!" Richard said. "I can't believe you're going to let a little thing like that scare you! That's all they were doing, you know." He shook his head and laughed. "I mean, please. Arson? Like lighting a bag on fire is arson. I'm not that dumb."

I just kept walking. He ran after me and gasped. "You *are* scared—aren't you?"

He was so annoying. I blew up at him. "Okay, so I'm scared! You happy now?"

Someone else said, "Scared of what?"

I turned around. It was Bebi. She was standing there with a Snack 'n Go bag in her arms, smiling at me.

"Oh…ah…nothing," I said.

Richard clapped me on the shoulder like I was the new Heavyweight Champion of the World.

"That's right," he said. "Emery Murray is afraid of nothing! The guy is incredibly brave. I'm talking fearless!"

I cringed, but Bebi laughed.

"That's good," she said. "I guess you won't be scared then when I tell you that my dad was ready to kill you! You should have seen him. He didn't believe that story about science camp for one minute..." She rolled her eyes. "That's my dad for you. He doesn't trust teenage boys *at all*."

"With a daughter like you, I can't blame him." Richard actually thought he was being smooth, but he just came across as cheesy. I could see Bebi was embarrassed. She looked away. She pushed this little strand of hair off her face and said, "Ah...so...where are you guys going?"

I shrugged and kind of nodded in the direction of our house.

"Is that where you live?" she said, pointing to Marjorie's.

"No," I said, "I live next door."

A whole sentence.

Wow. I actually said a whole sentence

to Bebi without stuttering, fainting or wetting my pants.

"Would you care to join us?" Richard said. He was still trying to do that smooth thing.

"Thanks, but I better get going." Bebi had these amazingly long eyelashes. "I've got Dad's milk. He needs it for his tea."

She walked away. Her hair came down way past the middle of her back. She turned around to wave and caught me staring at it. I must have looked like a perv.

I spun around and took off up our driveway. "See ya," I said to Richard.

"You're going?" he said. "What about our movie?"

"Look," I said, "I told you. I don't want to do it anymore. I don't care what you say. The cops scared me."

I thought he was going to make fun of me, but he didn't. He just said, "Fine.

If it's the arson thing that's bothering you, don't worry. We just won't do the fire part anymore."

I shrugged. "What's the point then? We already talked about that. It'll be boring without the fire."

"So? We'll come up with something else."

This was never going to work—and I was just as glad. "Like what?" I said. He followed me right up onto our front porch.

"We'll, um…"

He didn't have a clue. He looked around like he was going to find the answer in the shrubs or the flowerpots or the neighbor's curtains.

He clapped his hands together.

"We'll do it at night!" he said. "Like, three in the morning or something. It'll be pitch-dark out. We'll wake people up. They'll be all groggy and mad and everything. It'll be hysterical."

No doubt. That was just what the movie needed—more people wanting to kill us.

"There's a problem," I said. "I'm generally not allowed out at three in the morning—are you?"

He blew a blast of air out his mouth. "I can fix that!" he said. "You tell your mother you're staying at my place. I'll tell my mother I'm staying at yours. No one will ever know the difference. Piece of cake."

He was smiling away at me like one of those guys on TV who sells discount carpet. I knew no matter what I said, he'd have an answer for it.

"Okay, fine," I said. "We'll do it at night."

I was lying. I figured if I could lie to the cops, I could lie to Richard. It was an easy out. I'd phone him later and tell him my mother said I couldn't stay at his place. Not much he could do about that.

If I was lucky, by the next day he'd have given up on the whole stupid idea.

Unfortunately, right at that moment, my mother came barreling out of the house.

"Where are you going?" I said.

She squinted her eyes up and made this kind of "aargh" sound. "To the city! The Internet's down everywhere. I'm going to have to drive in if I want to get my article filed in time."

She wasn't happy about it, but she was doing her best not to go totally berserk while Richard was there. She scrambled into the car. She jabbed at the ignition about four times before she actually managed to get the key in.

"Put a frozen lasagna in the oven, would you? I'm not going to feel like making supper by the time I get back tonight."

Richard ran around and closed the car door as if he was her chauffeur or something.

"Mrs. Murray?" he said. "Would you mind if Emery stays over at my place tonight? We got a new Ping Pong table and…"

She was smiling, but I could tell she was anxious just to get out of there. She revved the engine a few times to keep the old clunker going and said, "Sure, Richard. As long as it's okay with your mother, it's fine with me."

She backed out. Richard waved and, without moving his lips, said, "Boy, she's even easier to manipulate than you are."

He elbowed me. "Just kidding."

Yeah. Right.

Door Number Six

Mom called from the car to say she wasn't coming home for dinner after all. She was frazzled after sitting in traffic for hours. She decided to stay in town and catch a play with her friend Cara.

That was fine by me. If she wasn't going to be there, I didn't have to bother eating any vegetables. I cut myself a piece of lasagna. I was hungry, but after a couple of bites I didn't feel like eating any more. I kept on thinking about Bebi—which was kind of nice—and Richard—which wasn't. How did he do it? Even when he wasn't around, he managed to weasel into my brain.

I had to get out of playing Nicky Nicky Nine Doors with him that night. I know I'd been telling myself that all day, but I was serious about it now. I truly hated the game. It was mean, it was stupid, it was dangerous and, worst of all, it was potentially embarrassing. If anyone I knew caught me playing, I'd never live it down.

It should have been so easy to pick up the phone and say I'm not going. But this was Richard I was dealing with. He wouldn't just say, "Sure. Whatever. No problem." One way or another he was going to talk me into playing again. I knew it. I could feel it in my stomach. It was like running a race with the world's fastest man or something. You know you're going to lose even before the starter's gun goes off. It kind of takes the fight out of you.

I tried not to let that bother me. I told myself, "Be a man. Call him. Tell him you quit." I'd get all revved up to phone, but somehow I always ended up putting it off. I guess I kept hoping something would happen. His mother wouldn't let him stay over, say, or a big thunderstorm would hit, or Richard would actually develop a conscience and decide he didn't want to do it either.

I scraped the rest of my lasagna into the compost bin and started playing video games instead. At least I knew how to defeat *those* enemy mutants.

That took my mind off things. I forgot about Nicky Nicky Nine Doors for a while. I have no idea how much time had gone by when the doorbell rang. I was sort of annoyed. The universe would have soon been mine. I got up anyway and opened the door.

Bebi must have thought I was an idiot. I just stood there staring at her with my tongue hanging out.

"Hi," she said.

She probably expected me to say "Hi" back—or to at least nod or blink or something.

She said, "You okay?" and looked at me in such a worried way I felt almost obliged to snap out of it. I gave my head a little shake to get my brain started up again.

"Yeah," I said. "I just, um…" I started searching for some reason to be acting so lame. I noticed something down the street. "Hey, look. An ambulance. Over there. Like, behind you."

I poked my head half out the door and tried to seem concerned instead of just stunned.

Bebi turned her head to see. Two men in blue uniforms were bringing

"Yeah," I said again. "Yeah. Good. Great. Yeah."

She slipped out the door. I had about an hour to improve my conversational skills.

a stretcher into Apron Guy's house. She put her hand over her mouth. "Oh no," she said. "It must be Norma. I hope she didn't die…Poor Bert. He's going to be so sad…"

Bebi kept talking about how Bert had quit his job to stay home and look after his sick wife, but I barely heard her. All I could think of was us ringing his stupid doorbell, dragging him out of the house and making fun of him in that apron. No wonder he was ready to murder us.

Bebi kind of pushed her way past me. "Ah, sorry. Do you mind if I come in?"

I must have nodded. She said, "Thanks" and closed the door. She peeked out the window. "My Dad would go insane if he caught me here. I'm not supposed to be alone with a boy."

Alone with a boy.

A boy.

I'm a boy. She's a girl. That made me gulp.

"Oh," I said. My face must have looked so weird.

"I probably shouldn't have come," she said. She turned away. I realized that she was as embarrassed as I was. She put her hand on the doorknob. "I better go."

"No," I said. "Don't go." I just kind of blurted it out, but it worked. She stopped. Her cheeks went all dark.

"Why are you here?" I said. It didn't come out the way I meant it to. I sounded like a principal who'd just caught a kid wandering the hallway during class time.

She looked at her hands and kind of laughed.

"Well, um…I have dance class tonight and, um…"

She stopped. Her eyes went all droopy. She took a big swallow. I knew exactly how she felt.

"Yeah?" I said.

"Well," she said, "I just maybe I could leave half an ho or so and we could, you know out together for a while, I mean want to or whatever." She said i big long sentence. Then she her lips into her mouth and sor them shut.

We both took a breath at the time.

Nicky Nicky Nine Doors with R didn't stand a chance anymore. " I said again and nodded my h whole bunch of times.

"Cool." She broke into thi smile. Her teeth were so white she have done a toothpaste comme "I'll sneak out at nine and meet here about ten minutes later. I told I was walking back with Stephanie Kuan-Yin. As long as I'm home by forty-five, he won't suspect anyth That sound good?"

Door Number Seven

I called Richard right away to say I couldn't meet him that night. Nobody was home so I hung up. I could have left a message, but I didn't. I was worried his parents might get suspicious.

I don't know if it was the excitement of having Bebi show up like that or nervousness about having to talk to

Richard, but something was making me feel sort of sick.

I turned off the computer and had a shower. I used my mother's razor to shave off the six whiskers I had growing on my chin. I should have just plucked them. What a hack job I did. I gave myself a big ugly gash and sliced the top off a pimple. I got blood all over my shirt. The only clean one I had was this white button-down thing Mom bought me for my grandfather's wedding. I put it on.

I looked like I was going to sing in the school choir. (No, I looked like I got beat up on my way to sing in the school choir.) I took it off. I went back to my old T-shirt. It was brown, so I figured once the blood dried it wouldn't show that much anyway. By the time I was ready, it was almost nine.

The doorbell rang.

I wondered if Bebi was early. This thought popped into my head: She just couldn't *wait* to see me. My heart went crazy. It was like I had a whole bunch of little animals inside me all randomly hurling themselves against my chest.

I checked my armpits. I did a quick look at myself in the hall mirror. I should have worn the clean shirt. Did the blood look gross? My chin was starting to get all scabby.

I told myself to relax. I smelled okay. Nothing I could do about a scabby chin now. I smiled into the mirror. At least there was no lasagna between my teeth.

I stood up straight to make myself look taller. I opened the door and said, "Hello."

No one was there. It appeared that Bebi *could* wait to see me after all.

I looked around, but it was dark. I couldn't see anyone. Not that I needed to see anyone. I knew immediately who must have rung my doorbell.

I went, "Richard!"

I stepped out onto the porch. I heard something move to my left. I turned my head.

Somebody grabbed me from behind.

Door Number Eight

I went, "Quit it, Richard! I mean it! Stop!" but even as I said it, I knew it wasn't him.

It couldn't be. He's too little. Whoever had me was way taller than Richard and stronger too.

I tried to scream, but all I got out was one sad little squeak before a hand covered my mouth from behind.

The person leaned in hard against my ear and went, "*Shhhh!*"

I tried to get away. I rammed my elbows back. I kicked. I threw my body around the way big fish do when they're trying to get off a line.

It didn't make any difference.

The person just held on tighter and kept hushing me. It was so creepy. It was like some really violent babysitter was trying to rock me to sleep.

I was terrified. I thrashed and thrashed until I realized it wasn't working. I was weak and getting weaker all the time. I had to do something else. Maybe if I pretended to cooperate, I could catch them off guard. I stopped struggling. We both just stood there panting for a few seconds. Then the person said, "Thank you," in this croaky voice.

Thank you? For what? For being a good victim?

It's weird, but that just made me mad. As if I'd give up that easily! What kind of a wuss did they take me for?

I lifted my leg and stomped down as hard as I could. My foot landed on a nice soft-toed sneaker.

I don't know if it was the pain or the shock, but it worked. There was a yelp, and suddenly I was free.

Too free.

With no one holding me back, I went flying forward. I tried to turn around and grab the railing, but I was too late. I fell backward down the steps.

I remember thinking this was really going to hurt, but I was wrong. I didn't feel anything.

I was out cold.

Someone was wiping my face with a wet cloth. I groaned. I opened my eyes. It was pitch-dark. I said, "Who's there?"

The person dropped the cloth and darted away. I heard a door shut and a lock click. I sat up. My head spun. I lay back down.

What was going on?

"Where am I?" My words sort of echoed.

I heard a noise, like someone laughing. I recognized the voice immediately. It made me so mad.

"Richard, you jerk!" I said. "Is this your idea of a joke? It isn't funny. Quit laughing!"

There was a long pause.

"I'm not laughing," he said. He sounded really small. "I've never been so scared in my life."

My whole body erupted into goose bumps. I realized this wasn't one of Richard's stupid pranks. Someone had got him too. We'd been kidnapped. Why?

My heart started pounding so hard it hurt.

I told myself to stay calm. I had to say it a few times before it sunk in at all. I clamped my teeth together to keep them from chattering.

I lay on the cold floor like that for a few minutes, too scared to move. I tried to blank out Richard's crying but I couldn't. It drilled right into me. He kept on crying until my brain finally got the message: Richard wasn't going to be any help. If I wanted to get out of there, I'd have to do it myself.

I took a deep breath. I got up on my hands and knees. I crawled in the direction of Richard's voice. The floor was smooth but really dusty. It left a chalky feeling on my hands.

I bumped into his body. I figured out where his shoulder was and gave him a little pat.

"We'll be okay, Richard. Don't worry." I heard him gulp. "We just need a plan." I said it in the cheery type of voice Mom always used after the divorce. It didn't fool me then, and I'm sure it wasn't fooling Richard now, but it was the best I could do.

"Do you know who was just here? The person wiping my face?" I said.

"No." Richard sniffed a few times. "It was too dark. I didn't see anything."

I had a headache. I ran my hand through my hair and felt a lump the size of a computer mouse.

"How did you get here?" I said.

"Someone grabbed me."

"The same person?"

"I don't know." He hesitated. "I didn't see. It was about eight thirty. I was getting some footage of the sun going down behind your house before I picked you up. I thought it would make a nice scene change between—"

I cut him off. "Richard. Forget about the stupid movie, would you?"

He went, "Sorry, sorry." There were tears in his voice again. I felt bad. I shouldn't have gotten mad at him.

"That's okay," I said. "Just tell me what happened next."

"Um. I'm not sure. It took me a long time to get the footage I wanted. I was looking through the camera, walking up to your house, and someone just jumped me from behind and dragged me here."

"Where's here?"

"I don't know!" He sucked in his breath. "Not far. Somewhere on the street maybe. I got confused. They covered my eyes. I kept falling down. I didn't know which way we were going."

"Did they say anything to you?"

"No. Well, yes. Sort of. They kept going, 'Shhh!'"

It had to be the same person.

"Do you think they're going to hurt us, Emery? Who would want to hurt *us*?"

I said, "Nobody." But the truth was I could think of lots of people.

Bert with the dying wife.

The Naked Guy.

That lady with the screaming babies.

Bebi's dad. She said he was ready to kill me. She might not have been joking after all.

The cops.

No. The cops wouldn't do this. The cops were going to save us! They'd realize we were gone and start a search. We were going to be okay.

I felt relieved for a second—then it hit me. I put my face in my hands.

The cops wouldn't even know we were missing! My mother thought I was at Richard's. His mother thought he was at my place. No one would notice we were gone until the next day. By then, it would be too late.

I was glad it was so dark. I didn't want Richard to see my face. He was upset enough as it was.

The door opened again. My heart slammed into my mouth. I stood up. "Please," I said, but the door closed before I could say anything more.

Someone else was here—and they were just as scared as I was. I could tell by their breathing. It was fast and squeaky and probably not doing much good.

"Who's there?" I said.

"Emery?"

It was Bebi. "Where are we?" she said. Her voice cracked.

I was just going to say, "I don't know," when the lights clicked on.

I didn't need to answer. We were clearly in someone's garage.

Bebi's hair was messy and her skin was gray. Richard was curled up on the floor next to a metal shelf full of bottled water and canned food. There wasn't much else in the place. A lawnmower. A plastic rake. A garbage can. It could have been anyone's garage around here. They were all the same. A big door to the outside. A little door to the house. No windows.

Bebi ran over and put her arms around me. Normally, that would have been nice. I couldn't help thinking, though, that if her father was behind this, I'd rather she just kept her distance.

"Someone grabbed me," she said.

I nodded. "Us too. Did you see who it was?" She put a hand over her mouth and shook her head. Watching her do that almost made me cry too. This was the scariest thing that had ever happened to me.

I sucked it up. "But you're okay?" I said.

She tried to smile.

"What about you, Richard?"

His face was pulled down into this frown, and his chin was trembling. "I'm all right," he said. He wiped his eyes with the back of his arm and stood up.

"Look," I said. "It's not so bad. There are three of us. We'll figure some way out of here."

It was obvious they didn't believe me. I just had to carry on anyway.

"Who's got a cell phone?" I said.

Amazing. Three teenagers and no cell phones. (They must have parents like mine.) So much for that idea.

I let go of Bebi and went over to the garage door. I turned the handle. It was locked. I rattled it up and down. I got everyone to ram their bodies against the door and scream as loud as they could. The door didn't move. Nobody came to rescue us. Did they not hear us scream— or did they just not care?

Bebi said, "Let's try pulling the door up from the bottom." We wedged our fingers underneath the rubber lip and heaved—but it was useless. The door wasn't going anywhere. We fell back onto the floor and tried to catch our breath.

After a while I said, "Okay. Let's try the other door now."

Nobody moved.

Bebi rubbed her teeth over her bottom lip. "I don't think that's a good idea," she said. "We don't know what's inside the house. It could be even worse in there."

She was right, but what choice did we have? We couldn't just sit there and wait for something to happen. I looked around for another way out. The place was like a dungeon. It was that door or nothing.

I saw the rake leaning against the wall. I walked over and picked it up. "Come on," I said. "We'll be okay."

Bebi looked at me for a couple of seconds before she stood up too. She grabbed a big bottle of water from the shelf. She held it upside down like a club. She handed a bottle to Richard and motioned for him to do the same.

We started walking to the door in single file. I wished I'd grabbed a water bottle instead of the rake. At least a water bottle would hurt if I had to hit someone with it.

We all heard the noise at the same time. We stopped dead. Someone was on the other side of the door, panting. Not panting the way a runner does after a marathon. This person was panting like a hungry animal about to tear apart a carcass.

Lot of good my little rake would do now. I put my arm around Bebi like I was trying to protect her, but who was I kidding? She must have felt me shaking.

Something shushed along the floor. It wasn't very loud, but we all jumped as if a hand grenade had gone off.

A sheet of paper slid under the door.

We stared at it for a few seconds. I let go of Bebi, picked it up, raced back and put my arm around her again. I don't know if it made her feel better, but it helped me.

Are you all right? was written in big purple letters.

Bebi crinkled up her face and whispered, "Weird." I was thinking the same thing. You don't expect your kidnapper to ask how you're doing. (If they really cared, they wouldn't have dragged us here in the first place.)

Thinking that kind of twigged something in my brain. Maybe this wasn't what it seemed. Maybe there was some hope after all. I had an idea.

I whispered, "Do you have anything to write with?"

Bebi patted her pockets and then shook her head. The only thing Richard had was a chocolate bar. I squinted at him. What was he doing with stunt poo? My guess is he'd been planning some late-night fires after all.

I took the bar and peeled back the wrapper. I flipped the note over and scratched out an answer with it. The chocolate smudged a bit, but you could still read it. *Yes,* I wrote. *R U?* Somehow it just seemed safer to write an answer than say it.

Richard and Bebi looked at me like "What are you doing?" It was a long shot. Someone had wiped my face, turned on the light and sent us the note. Maybe the person wasn't as bad as we thought. Or maybe the bad guy had gone and left us with someone else—someone good. I decided to appeal to their better nature. As far as I could tell, it was our only way out of there.

I pushed the note under the door. Ten seconds later, a new sheet of paper came back. It said, *I am now. Thank you.*

I could feel my heart slowing to a normal rate. Whoever was guarding us was at least polite. That seemed like a good sign.

I wrote back, *U weren't B4?*

The answer took a while to come. *No. I was scared.*

I tried to reply, but the bar crumbled in my hand. I wanted to keep communicating.I had the feeling that's what would save us.

"Um, sorry," I said out loud. "I can't answer you. My chocolate bar ran out."

The person laughed. Bebi squeezed my hand. Richard's eyebrows shot up. You could feel us all relax a bit.

"What were you afraid of?" I said.

There was shuffling on the other side of the door. The person coughed a few times and then whispered, "You."

"Me? Us?" I said.

"Uh-huh."

I looked at Richard. Those fires had been *such* a bad idea.

I started to narrow down who our kidnapper could be. We didn't use a fire with Bert. We used one with the lady, but she didn't seem scared. She didn't even try to put it out. I realized now too it couldn't be Bebi's dad. He wouldn't abduct his own daughter.

I mouthed the words, "It's Naked Guy."

"Why were you afraid of us?" I said. I tried to sound innocent.

The voice was sort of stumbling and higher than I expected it to be. "I watched you all day…I watched your game… I knew sooner or later you were going to come for me."

I shook my head at Richard. We both knew immediately it couldn't be Naked Guy. We'd already got *him*.

Who was it?

The person was getting more and more agitated. "Then today, I heard you talking on your porch. You said you were coming tonight."

Our porch? Who could have heard us talking on our porch?

I looked at all the water, the canned food. I thought of the curtains moving, someone watching us. It was a hot day. Windows would be open.

The answer kind of washed over me. I suddenly knew it wasn't a man at all.

It was Marjorie.

A sick old lady had caught us. It didn't make sense—but who else could it be? Did she have a helper? What did she do all day in her house? I tried to think if any other kids had gone missing.

Then I tried not to think about it. It was too creepy.

Her voice was getting louder and faster. She was panting again.

"I knew I'd have to come outside…," she said. "I'd have to put the fire out… What if someone saw me? What if…?"

She started making the type of whimpering noise dogs make when they want to be let in.

"We weren't going to ring your doorbell!" I said. "Honest. We really weren't."

I could hear her trying to get her breathing back under control.

"Are you all right, Marjorie?" I said. "Would you like some water?"

"No, thank you. You're very kind," she said. She obviously forgot it was her own water I was offering her.

She paused.

"I'm sorry I did this to you," she said. "I didn't mean to hurt you. I…I just… panicked."

She had to stop again and calm herself down.

"As you may have guessed," she said after a while, "I have a condition…a phobia. A fear of the outside. I get panic attacks. I can't control them."

Richard had been quiet, but now he suddenly felt the need to pipe up. "If you were so afraid of the outside, how come you came out and kidnapped us?" I kicked his leg. Was he nuts? Why get her riled up now? That's all we needed.

"Good point!" She laughed, but when she spoke again she was serious. "Tonight I saw one of you boys pointing the camera at my house. You did it for the longest time. My anxiety skyrocketed. I felt like a trapped animal. You were coming to get me! I was overcome by panic. I had no choice. I had to get to you before you got me."

We could hear her moving her feet around. "I couldn't bear the thought of you seeing me, so I snuck up on you from behind. I realize that was a mistake and that of course you'd be frightened, but I wasn't thinking straight. I was only going to ask you to leave me alone, but you screamed and tried to get away. I was so terrified that I dragged you in here."

I had to ask. "Why did you come for me too then?" I said. "You rang my doorbell."

"Because you were in it together! You'd notice he was gone, you'd come after me…" She moaned. "I'm sorry. I'm sorry about your head, about everything. I really am. I used to be a nurse, so I was pretty sure you were okay. But I was also sure that I'd got myself into a terrible mess now. I knew I had to call the authorities, but I was too scared to pick up the phone. I was pacing by the window wondering what to do when I saw the girl. I remembered her talking with you today, staring at my house. I had to grab her too! This whole thing was snowballing out of control. I know it sounds crazy, but…but…"

I'm not sure if she was laughing or crying. "But I guess I *am* crazy. Who would keep themselves locked up in a house for five years if they weren't crazy?"

"You're not crazy," I said. "We shouldn't have been playing that stupid game. We bugged a lot of people. I bet you're not the only person who wanted to kill us."

"I didn't want to kill you!" she said.

I didn't have time to explain that it was just a figure of speech. The doorbell rang.

I heard her gasp.

"Oh no!" she whispered. "There's a police car here!"

Her breathing started going nuts again.

Marjorie whispered, "They're coming to get me! They know what I've done! They're going to take me downtown!

They'll put my picture in the paper! Everyone will see me!"

The doorbell rang again.

We heard Marjorie begin to rock back and forth. She seemed to be humming or something.

There was a loud knock on the door. A man's voice said, "Open up! Police!"

"Please," Marjorie whispered. "Help me. Don't make me talk to them." She was begging. "Tell them what I did. Please. Please."

"Don't worry," I said. "We'll help you. You hide. We'll talk to the cops."

Marjorie unlocked the door.

She disappeared by the time we'd stepped into the house.

Door Number Nine

I opened the front door.

"Hello, Officer," I said. "Is there a problem?"

It was the same cop we saw before. He looked at me like "*You* again!" Then he saw Bebi and smiled.

"Not anymore," he said. "Seems like we found our missing girl. This you,

Miss?" He pulled a photo out of his pocket and showed it to her.

She nodded.

"Your father's very worried about you," he said. "You're going to have some explaining to do." Bebi's face went pale. I got the feeling she'd rather be kidnapped again than have to face her dad. She squeezed my hand. I was worried I'd never get to see her again once her dad found out what happened.

"This is all my fault, Officer." The voice surprised us. We turned around to see Marjorie walking down the hall.

She was big and tall and very pale, but she wasn't old. Thirty-five or forty, maybe. She had this quivery smile on her face.

"I shouldn't have kept the girl so long," she said. "I haven't been feeling well. The kids were helping me."

The officer winked. "Maybe you'd like to tell her dad that. He might not be so hard on her then."

I could feel how nervous that made Marjorie. "Sure," she said. She cleared her throat. "There's one more thing too. Would you mind driving me to the hospital on your way back? I think it's time I saw somebody about…my condition."

She rubbed her hands together and swallowed. "You might like to talk to me about a few things too," she said.

"No problem," the cop said. "We can chat in the car after we drop Bebi off. Now, why don't you boys run along home?"

I turned to Bebi. "See you tomorrow?" I said hopefully.

Her face still looked scared, but her eyes lit up a bit. "Yeah," she said. "That would be nice."

The cop tapped his foot. I got the feeling he didn't trust teenage boys any more than her father did. I gave Bebi's hand another squeeze, and then Richard and I headed down the stairs.

"Boys?" We turned back around. Marjorie was rubbing her fingers together as if she was trying to get something sticky off them.

My heart started thumping. I didn't know what she was going to say. It's weird. She was the one who kidnapped us but I still felt guilty. Marjorie was going to be in a lot of trouble all because we got bored one day and decided to play some stupid game. I wanted to apologize to her but I didn't know where to start.

She looked at me in a way that made me think I didn't have to. She said, "I certainly hope I'll bump into you on the street some time soon."

It's funny—but that made me feel kind of better.

I watched her step out the door.

I'm pretty sure she smiled as she closed it behind her.

As she got in the car, Richard elbowed me in the ribs and whispered, "I told you Nicky Nicky Nine Doors would be fun."

Vicki Grant is a bestselling and award-winning author of many books for juveniles and young adults, including *I.D.* and *Dead-End Job* in the Orca Soundings series and *Pigboy* in the Orca Currents series, all of which were ALA Quick Picks. Her comic legal thriller for teens, *Quid Pro Quo,* won the Arthur Ellis Award for Best Juvenile Crime Fiction. Vicki lives in Halifax, Nova Scotia. Visit her website at www.vickigrant.com.

orca *currents*

The following is an excerpt from
another exciting Orca Currents novel,
The Snowball Effect by Deb Loughead.

978-1-55469-370-2 $9.95 pb
978-1-55469-371-9 $16.95 lib

Dylan and his friends cause
a car accident when they pack snowballs with rocks
and throw them at a passing car. When his friends
flee, Dylan goes to the scene of the accident to
make sure the driver is okay. Dylan is sighted and,
rather than being punished, he is lauded as a
hero. As his lies pile up, so does the hype about his
heroics and his fear of being exposed.

Chapter One

On Friday evening when Garrett called, I was in the mood for anything. I had my parka and my snow boots ready at the door. By six o'clock I was going antsy waiting for that call. I didn't want to spend the rest of the evening at home with my grandma. Gran was desperate for someone to play cards with her.

After three games of gin rummy, I needed to get out of the apartment.

"We're on at Matt's for tonight," he told me. "You in?"

"Of course," I said. "The usual Friday-night feast. Wouldn't miss it!"

"Don't forget your balaclava," Garrett added. "For *after* the feast. You're sticking around for *that* too, right? You're not backing out on us, are ya, Dillweed?"

My stomach twisted, and I paused.

"Well?" Garrett said. "Can we count on you or what?"

I hesitated for only a second. I didn't like to keep this guy waiting. "Yeah sure. I guess I'm in. See ya in fifteen," I told him. Then I started hauling on my winter gear.

"If you're going out, can you pick me up a bag of Cheezies at the gas station?" Gran called from the kitchen, where she was playing a game of solitaire.

"Sure thing, Gran," I told her. "I'll grab some cash out of the sugar bowl."

Mom left some of her tip money for me and Gran to use whenever we needed it. She usually came home with some great tips from Rocky's Roadhouse, where she worked as a bartender. Wintertime brought in the best tips of all. The curlers dropped by on their way to the arena, or on their way home, and knocked back some pints. Hockey players stopped in too, after their games. In Bridgewood everything was within walking distance, and nobody worried about drinking and driving.

The exception was the snowmobilers. Those guys spent most of their free time riding snowmobiles on the trails that snaked through Bridgewood and cut a swath through the surrounding forests. They were decent guys, mostly, and Mom knew the law. She cut them off before they could be over the legal limit, and they respected her judgment.

"Make sure they're the good kind, not the no-name brand, okay," my grandma called. "I can't stand those cheap cheesy Cheezies. Ha!" She laughed out loud at her joke. "Get it, Dylan?"

"Yeah, I get it, Gran," I told her. "Hope you're not in a hurry though. I probably won't be home till eleven thirty or so."

"That's okay. I'll be waiting up for your mom anyway. There's a good movie starting at midnight, so I can just eat 'em then."

"See ya later, Gran," I called over my shoulder as I slammed out the door.

I ran all the way down the six flights of stairs instead of waiting for the elevator. When I burst through the front doors, I was punched in the nose by the windchill. My nostrils froze instantly. But the balaclava did a great job of protecting the rest of my face. The snow was crunchy underfoot. It was like walking on soda crackers. Winter had already set in with a vengeance, and it was only the beginning of December.

In this part of the country, Old Man Winter sinks his teeth in early and stays late. Usually by November he's settled in for the long haul. We get lake-effect snow, which happens when cold wind scoops moisture off the warmer lake water and dumps snow on us. A few inches of snow can fall in an hour. It's like living in a snow globe that someone's constantly shaking. Sure it's pretty. Pretty annoying! But we're used to it around here. We find plenty to do for fun on a Friday night in the ice-cold darkness.

Overhead the stars were bright pinpoints in the sky, the moon barely a toenail clipping. For a change there weren't any streamers of snow pouring off the lake tonight. I hurried along the sidewalk, sliding on patches of ice the way I always did. It was the closest I ever came to skating. Not having a dad to teach me or a mom who could afford the equipment, I'd never even learned to skate properly.

I knew how hard it was for Mom to scrape up cash for groceries and the bills, even with the help of Gran's pension. So I didn't complain much. Now that I was fifteen, it was embarrassing to go to the ice rink and have all my friends, guys *and* girls, zoom past while I hung on to the boards. I avoided that rink.

The closer I got to Matt's place, the louder my stomach grumbled. I could practically hear it talking to me through my jacket. Hanging out at Matt's was always the best part of Friday night. Matt's parents were really cool, especially his dad. He liked to play pool with us, or sometimes even poker. He loved cooking too, and he always made the four of us his sous-chefs.

When I got there, I walked right through the back door without knocking. Their door was never locked. I tore off all my winter clothes and nearly sprinted to the kitchen. The guys were all gathered around the counter as usual. Garrett, Matt and Cory each had a task to do. Matt's mom was sitting at the table sipping a glass of wine while she watched the show.

"About time, Dillweed," Garrett said. "I planned on scarfing down all yours if you didn't show up soon to help."

Matt and Cory laughed along with Garrett. I cringed, because I knew he probably meant it.

"Don't worry, I would have saved you some," Matt's dad said with a huge grin. He was a big guy with sandy hair and a wicked sense of humor. "I need you here on Friday nights. You're my chief cheese grater, you know. Wash your hands, buddy, 'cause it's pizza night and the oven's hot."

He handed me the block of cheese and the grater after I dried my hands. "Okay, get to work, Dylan," he said, then started rolling out pizza dough.

"How come Dylan always gets to grate?" Garrett said, struggling to chop the onions. "I hate doing onions. They always make my eyes water."

"Because Dylan's such a machine," Matt's dad told us. "Jeez, don't *cry* about it, Garrett" He added, then passed him a box of tissues.

We all snickered.

"Hah, that's just hilarious," Garrett said. He glowered at me, like he wished he was being called a machine instead of me. "My eyes are actually burning, you know."

"Oh, you'll survive," Matt's dad said, patting him on the back. "Suck it up, bub!"

"Yeah, you think chopping's hard. I get stuck pitting these olives," Matt complained. "It's impossible. Why don't we have the pitted ones this time?"

"And these disgusting anchovies totally reek." Cory grimaced as he tried to twist off the tin lid.

"Ever smelled Matt's hockey bag? Trust me, those anchovies are *roses*," Matt's dad said. "Boy, you guys are whining like little girls tonight. What's up with that?"

I laughed out loud.

"But, Dad, this is taking forever and we're all starving," Matt said as he carefully pried out another olive pit.

"Well, don't drool all over the veggies and cheese, boys," his dad warned us. "Mom doesn't like extra sauce on her pizza."

"Okay, that's *gross*," Matt's mom said, rolling her eyes. "I guess I just don't get your goofy guy humor. And I think I just lost my appetite too."

"Great, my plan worked! More for us," Matt's dad said, and we all cracked up.

orca currents

For more information on all the books
in the Orca Currents series, please visit
www.orcabook.com.